GENERAL SERIES 101

Modern Greece

RICHARD CLOGG

The Historical Association
59a Kennington Park Road, London SE11 4JH

ACKNOWLEDGEMENTS

The cover photograph on the front and back outside cover depicts the last Emperor of Byzantium, Constantine XI Palaiologos, fighting alongside his troops during the final assault on Constantinople by the Ottoman Turks on 29 May 1453. It was painted by Theophilos [Khatzimikhail], 1867-1934. The map on page 4 is reproduced from *A Short History of Modern Greece* by Richard Clogg, 1979 by permission of the publisher Cambridge University Press and the author.

© Richard Clogg, 1981
ISBN 0 85278 244 6
H.A. 9.5-5-81
Printed in Great Britain by
Hart-Talbot Printers Ltd.,
Saffron Walden

Contents

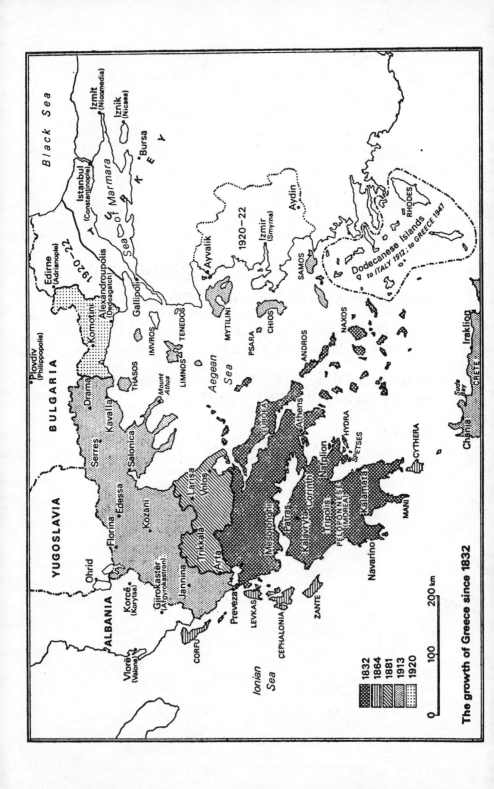

The growth of Greece since 1832

Black Sea

Izmit (Nicomedia)
Iznik (Nicaea)
Bursa

Istanbul (Constantinople)
Edirne (Adrianople)
Sea of Marmara
T U R K E Y
Gallipoli
Alexandroupolis (Dedeagatch)
Komotini
1920-22

Plovdiv (Philippopolis)
BULGARIA
Drama
Kavalla
Serres
Salonica
Edessa
Florina
Kozani

Ayvalik
Izmir (Smyrna)
Aydin
1920-22

SAMOS
MYTILINI
CHIOS
PSARA

RHODES
Dodecanese Islands
to ITALY 1912; to GREECE 1947

YUGOSLAVIA
Ohrid
ALBANIA
Korcë (Korytsa)
Gjirokastër (Argyrokastron)
Vlorë (Valona)
Jannina
Preveza

IMVROS
LIMNOS
TENEDOS
THASOS
Mount Athos

Aegean Sea

NAXOS
ANDROS

Larisa
Volos
Trikkala
Arta

EUBOEA
Athens
HYDRA
SPETSES
Mesolonghi
Patras
Corinth
Kalavryta
Tripolis
Nauplion
PELOPONNESE (MOREA)
Kalamata
MANI
Navarino

CYTHERA

Suda Bay
Chania
Iraklion
CRETE

LEVKAS
CEPHALONIA
CORFU
ZANTE

Ionian Sea

1832
1864
1881
1913
1920

0   100   200 km

Introduction

In January 1981, with her accession as the tenth member of the European Economic Community, Greece was 'legitimised' as a European country. The decision to join the EEC was not without challenge in Greece itself, and Greeks will doubtless continue to speak of 'travelling to Europe' as though their own country were not, in fact, European. Greece's entry into the EEC nevertheless represents one of the most momentous undertakings in the century and a half since she gained her independence in the early eighteen-thirties. The decision of the Nine to admit Greece to full membership also represents a significant stage in the development of the Community, for not only is Greece economically the least developed of the member states, but her historical experience and cultural heritage differ radically from those of the existing nine members. More than four hundred years of Ottoman rule, together with the legacy of Orthodox Christianity, have left their distinctive impress on the development of Greek society. Protestant and Catholic Europe are heirs to a common historical tradition of which Greece, with the rest of the Orthodox world, has had no part. Great historical movements such as the Renaissance, the Reformation, the Counter-Reformation, the seventeenth century scientific revolution, the Enlightenment, the French Revolution, and the Industrial Revolution have very largely passed her by.

Although the recent historical experience of Greece has been very different from that of her new European partners, her former history and culture have had a profound influence on the development of European civilization. Politicians, in welcoming Greece into Europe, have frequently paid obeisance to this great heritage. In the House of Commons, for instance, a Foreign Office Minister declared that Greece's forthcoming entry would be seen as 'a fitting repayment by the Europe of today of the cultural and political debt that we all owe to a Greek heritage almost 3,000 years old'. Yet to Greeks themselves the burden of the past has proved to be a mixed blessing. From the very beginnings of the independent state, *progonoplexia*, or ancestoritis, has distorted the country's cultural and educational life and inhibited the natural development of the language. Moreover, the heritage of a universally admired past has led to an undue neglect of the modern history of Greece. For centuries, the Western world has expended great effort in eluci- dating the language and civilization of ancient Greece. During the last hundred years the study of Greece's medieval, or 'Byzantine', Empire has developed remarkably. Only in the past few decades, outside Greece at least, has the academic study of the history, society and culture of modern Greece reached 'take-off' stage.

The reasons for this are several. With the establishment of com- munist régimes elsewhere in the Balkan peninsula in the aftermath of World War II, and with the narrow defeat of communist insurgency in Greece itself, the country came to occupy a pivotal role in the development of the Cold War. Greece's new political and strategic significance lent the study of her history and politics a greater relevance and even urgency to the western world. Civil war was followed, between 1967 and 1974, by the Colonels' dictatorship, a humiliating episode which provoked many Greeks to seek an understanding of the historical roots of their predicament. Outside Greece the Colonels' dictatorship provoked a flood of literature, much of it polemical in tone, but some of it of enduring value. Meanwhile, the many tourists that descended on Greece in the 1960s and 1970s helped to stimulate an interest in the life and culture of the latter day descendants of those worthies of ancient Greece whose physical remains dot the landscape. More recently, the prospect of Greek entry into the EEC has further helped focus attention on the country's politics, economy and society. Yet despite this remarkable expansion in the field of modern Greek studies, whole areas of the modern history of the Greek people await serious research and analysis.

Since Greece gained her independence in 1832, she has experienced an unusually troubled history which has distorted her political, economic and social development in a number of ways. Following the civil war that wracked the country in the nineteen- forties, she has experienced a rate of economic and social change of truly astonishing proportions. One of the reasons for the political instability that has characterised the post-war period, culminating in the Colonels' dictatorship between 1967 and 1974, has been the failure to develop institutions capable of responding to this rapidly accelerating pace of economic growth and social transformation. It remains to be seen whether Greece's accession to the EEC will contribute to the consolidation of democratic institutions and speed up the process of modernization, as the protagonists of Greek entry maintain. It is hoped, however, that the brief and necessarily selective survey of the modern history of Greece which follows will go some way, at least, towards explaining such distinctive, and at times puzzling, features of Greek society as political clientelism, the factionalism of political life, and the chronic tendency of the military to intervene in the political process.

The Ottoman Legacy

The Greeks were the first of the subject peoples of the Ottoman Empire to develop an articulated national movement and to secure an independent and (in theory at least) sovereign existence. The Serbs had rebelled earlier, but had obtained only quasi-autonomous status in 1815. Greek nationalism was, moreover, as Elie Kedourie has pointed out (*Nationalism in Asia and Africa* (1971), p.42), the first 'to appear outside Western Christendom, among a community ruled by non-Christians, and itself hitherto violently hostile to all Western notions'. The example set by the Greeks in overthrowing Ottoman rule was to be followed later in the 19th century by the Romanians, Bulgarians and Albanians, but the Bulgarian and Albanian national movements were directed as much against Greek ecclesiastical and cultural pretensions as against Ottoman oppression. By the first decades of the nineteenth century Greek society was a great deal more socially differentiated than that of any of the other Balkan peoples, and this partly explains why the Greeks were able in 1821 to launch their hazardous but ultimately successful revolt against Ottoman rule. One major reason for this distinctive (at least in the Balkan context) configuration of Greek society is to be found in the means by which the Ottoman Turks sought to govern the non-Muslim peoples of their vast multi-confessional and heteroglot Empire, the *millet* system.

With the consolidation of their power in South Eastern Europe in the fifteenth century the Ottomans were faced with the problem of governing very substantial non-Muslim populations. This they overcame by devolving a considerable degree of autonomy upon the various religious groupings in the Empire, a practice very much in accordance with Islamic tradition. Each *millet*, or 'nation', embraced all the members of a given religion, irrespective of ethnic origin. There was thus a Muslim *millet*, an Armenian *millet*, a Jewish *millet*, a Catholic *millet* and even, in the nineteenth century, a small Protestant *millet*. Apart from the Muslim *millet*, much the largest was the *Millet-i Rum* or 'Greek' *millet*. The *Millet-i Rum* embraced, besides Greeks, all the Orthodox Christian inhabitants of the Empire, be they Bulgarians, Serbs, Romanians, Vlachs, Orthodox Albanians or Arabs.

7

Just as the *Millet-i Rum* enjoyed a precedence over the other non-Muslim *millets*, so the Greeks enjoyed a dominant position within it. The head of the *millet*, the Ecumenical Patriarch of Constantinople, was always a Greek, and Greeks dominated the hierarchy of the Orthodox Church, through which the *millet* was administered. Greek control of the patriarchates of Alexandria, Jerusalem, and Antioch was strengthened by their financial dependence on Constantinople, while the suppression, at the instigation of the Holy Synod in Constantinople, of the Serbian patriarchate of Péc in 1766 and of the Bulgarian archbishopric of Ohrid in 1767 further increased the Greek stranglehold over the affairs of the Orthodox *millet*.

The powers enjoyed by the Ecumenical Patriarch were very extensive, and embraced, besides strictly religious matters, the power to raise taxation and exercise jurisdiction over a wide range of civil matters, e.g. inheritance and debt. The concession of such wide-ranging authority to the Patriarch by the Ottoman sultans assumed as a *quid pro quo* that he would act as guarantor of the loyalty of his flock. The execution of the Patriarch Gregory V on the outbreak of the Greek revolt in 1821, and this despite the fact that he had denounced the insurgents in the strongest of terms, was seen in Europe as an act of wanton savagery; but in Ottoman eyes Gregory had failed in his primary duty, that of ensuring the political obedience of his people.

The great powers enjoyed by the Church under Ottoman rule had a number of consequences. One was that in many areas of the Empire Orthodox Christians had much more contact with their own ecclesiastical authorities than they did with their Ottoman overlords, and the exactions of the Church came increasingly to be resented by Greeks and even more by non-Greeks, for whom Greek ecclesiastical hegemony often resulted in linguistic and cultural insensitivity. Another was that such a concentration of power occasioned fierce rivalries among candidates for the patriarchate. So sought after was the office that one 18th century patriarch, Kallinikos III, is reported to have expired of joy on hearing the news of his election. It was not long before an enormous *peshkesh* or bribe was payable to the Grand Vizir on each occasion that the office of patriarch changed hands. The Ottomans thus had a vested interest in a rapid turn over, and in the seventeenth century alone the office of Ecumenical Patriarch changed hands fifty-eight times, the average tenure of office being some twenty months. Although a patriarch theoretically enjoyed his position for life, it was by no means unusual for an individual to lose and regain office on more than one occasion. Dionysios IV Mouselimis, for instance, was five times patriarch between 1671 and 1694. Small wonder that an Armenian ('a banker but honest for all that') reproached an eighteenth century chronicler with the jibe that the Greeks changed their patriarchs more often than their shirts. Corruption became firmly rooted at all levels of the hierarchy, and the exactions and venality of the Church contributed to the development of a powerful strain of popular anti-clericalism. This was reinforced among the intelligentsia by the hierarchy's willingness to act as an apologist for the continuance of Ottoman hegemony. In 1798, for instance, a Patriarch of Jerusalem argued that the Ottoman Empire was of divine creation and had been specifically raised up to protect Orthodoxy from contamination by the Catholic West.

During the early centuries after the fall of Constantinople the energies of the Greeks were largely concentrated on physical survival. Towards the end of the seventeenth century, however, Greek society began to change in a number of significant ways, and by the end of the eighteenth century the Greeks had come to enjoy a degree of economic prosperity, cultural awareness, and political power unmatched by any of the non-Muslim peoples of the Ottoman Empire. In part this was a consequence of Ottoman decline, and of the Empire's gradual retreat from its European provinces and from the northern shores of the Black Sea as a result of Austrian and Russian pressure. No longer could the Porte, as in the centuries when the Empire's power was at its zenith, simply dictate to its adversaries. Skilled diplomats were needed, and these were found among the Phanariot Greeks. Drawn from a tightly knit group of some eleven families from the Phanar quarter of Constantinople, the Phanariots, from the end of the seventeenth century until the outbreak of the Greek revolt in 1821, monopolised the post of *Terdjuman bashi*, or principal interpreter to the Porte, an office whose functions in the conduct of the Empire's foreign relations were much wider than the title might imply. Phanariot Greeks also came to control the office of interpreter to the *kapudan pasha*, the commander of the Ottoman fleet. This carried with it the *de facto* governorship of the islands of the Aegean, from whose Greek inhabitants a large part of the crews of the imperial navy were drawn. In the eighteenth century Phanariots also came to monopolise the post of *hospodar,* or prince, of the Danubian Principalities of Moldavia and Wallachia, which under Ottoman suzerainty enjoyed a considerable degree of autonomy. Competition for these offices was intense, and huge bribes were used to secure the princely thrones of Jassy or Bucharest. But the rewards were correspondingly great, and a number of Phanariot princes managed to amass vast fortunes before their usually brief reigns were abruptly terminated by the intrigues of their rivals. The Phanariots acquired a reputation for rapacity which was certainly in part justified, but some of them introduced important reforms and acted as patrons of (Greek) education and culture. Moreover, through its tradition of service to the Porte in some of the highest offices of the state, this Phanariot *noblesse de robe* acquired a degree of political experience that was subsequently to stand the Greeks in good stead.

Undoubtedly the most important development in Greek society during the eighteenth century was the emergence of a powerful and prosperous mercantile bourgeoisie, engaged, somewhat paradoxically, as much without as within the Ottoman dominions. In the early centuries of Ottoman rule, Armenians and Jews had played the dominant role in the commerce of the Empire. For reasons that have yet to be adequately explained, the Greeks now took over this role, with the result that, as Professor Dakin has observed, they in effect came to control a commercial empire before they had achieved political independence (D. Dakin, 'The Greek Unification and the Italian Risorgimento compared', *Balkan Studies*, x (1969) p.7). By the end of the eighteenth century Greek entrepreneurs controlled much of the trade of the Ottoman Empire, and were quick to exploit the absence of an indigenous mercantile class in territories such as Hungary and the northern shores of the Black Sea that had been reconquered from the Ottomans. Greek merchants were active throughout the Mediterranean and Central Europe, and in the eighteenth century they established mercantile colonies in areas as widely dispersed as New Smyrna in Florida (a disastrous failure) and Bengal (a conspicuous success). Much of the carrying trade of the Empire, the export of raw materials and the import of manufactured goods and colonial produce, was conducted in Greek ships, and a thriving mercantile marine developed in the islands of Hydra, Spetses, and Psara. Greek shipowners made vast profits running the blockade during the period of the French revolutionary and Napoleonic wars. Many of these merchant ships were armed against pirates, and this nautical tradition proved a great asset to the Greeks during the war of independence.

The Greek mercantile presence has sometimes been exaggerated, due to the tendency of some contemporary observers to lump together hellenised Vlachs, Orthodox Albanians, and even Serbs, Bulgarians, and Romanians as 'Greeks' (a tendency encouraged by the fact that Greek was the *lingua franca* of Balkan commerce); but the existence of a dynamic and prosperous merchant class is not in dispute. More problematical is the contribution of the merchants to the development of the national movement. It has been argued that these merchants, frustrated by the arbitrariness, inefficiency, and increasing lawlessness of the Empire, were moved to support the struggle against Ottoman rule so as to establish a state that would be much less inimical to the creation and retention of wealth. It is true that many Greek merchants did admire the ordered societies of the West, where the state gave positive encouragement to the development of trade. But it is not clear whether they were prepared to jeopardise their comfortable niche in the existing Ottoman social fabric by aiding and abetting seemingly foolhardy schemes for national liberation. Certainly contemporary nationalist polemic frequently paints an unflattering picture of the wealthy members of the mercantile *diaspora* as being uninterested in the fate of their *patrida*, or motherland, and concerned only with the accumulation of money.

However, one way in which the mercantile bourgeoisie did undoubtedly contribute to the development of the national movement was by underwriting the remarkable upsurge in intellectual activity that characterised the Greek world in the seventy years or so before 1821. In keeping with the intense local patriotism that has been an enduring feature of Greek society, merchants endowed schools and libraries in their home communities and funded scholarships for study in the universities of Western Europe. It was these students, frequently themselves the offspring of merchants, who, upon coming into contact with the intoxicating ideas of the European Enlightenment and of the French Revolution, articulated what has been termed the 'Neo-Hellenic Enlightenment'. This manifested itself in a number of ways: in a notable growth in Greek printing (almost all of it carried on outside the confines of the Empire); in the reinvigoration of education; in a revival of interest in philosophy and the natural sciences; and, above all, in a new awareness by the nascent intelligentsia of a sense of their Hellenic ancestry, a conviction that they were heirs to a cultural heritage that was universally admired in the civilised world. It was, for instance, during the first decade of the nineteenth century that Greeks began the practice of naming their children (and their ships) after the worthies of ancient Greece.

A key role in instilling into the Greeks a consciousness of their heritage was played by Adamantios Korais, a native of Smyrna, who, having failed to make the grade as a merchant in Amsterdam, studied medicine at Montpellier, and established himself in Paris in 1788 as a classical scholar and publicist. From there until his death in 1833 Korais bombarded his fellow countrymen with nationalist polemic and editions of the Greek classics, prefaced by improving exhortations in which he urged his fellow countrymen to cast off the monkish barbarism into which they had fallen and to imitate the French in all things. For he believed that, among modern Europeans, it was the French who most closely reflected the virtues of the ancient Greeks. Without ever being very specific he believed that education would somehow necessarily bring in its wake political emancipation. This intellectual fervour did not go unchallenged within Greece, particularly on the part of the Church, which feared that Western learning and the renewed interest in the ancient world could only lead to atheism or, what was perhaps worse, Popery.

By 1800 then, Greek society was undergoing a process of rapid change. Increasing numbers of Greeks were developing a sense of national consciousness and finding the continuance of Ottoman rule ever more intolerable. Unfortunately many of the richest, most powerful, and best educated elements in society, the merchants, the Phanariots, the hierarchs of the church, and the *kodjabashis* or provincial notables, were manifestly disinclined to upset the Ottoman *status quo*. The great mass of the Greek people, the peasants, were largely indifferent to the nationalist obsessions of the intelligentsia, even if a primitive form of national feeling was inherent in their almost universal subscription to prophecies and oracles foretelling an eventual liberation by divine rather than human intervention from the Hagaren yoke. Throughout the period of Ottoman rule there were sporadic revolts, and the *klephts*, or bandits, with their attacks on such visible symbols of Ottoman authority as tax collectors, afforded an example of pre-nationalist armed resistance; but it was not until the end of the eighteenth century that plans for co-ordinated rebellion against the Ottoman yoke began to evolve.

The Struggle for Independence, 1800–1827

The lead in elaborating concrete plans for an armed struggle for independence was taken by Rigas Velestinlis (Pheraios), a Thessalian Vlach who had served the Phanariot rulers of the Danubian Principalities. In Vienna during the early seventeen-nineties he had been profoundly influenced by the doctrines of the French Revolution, an influence which was directly manifested in the *Declaration of the Rights of Man* and the *New Political Constitution of the Inhabitants of Rumeli, Asia Minor, the Islands of the Aegean and the Principalities of Moldavia and Wallachia* which he had printed in Vienna in the form of revolutionary tracts. With these he set off in 1797 to stir up a Balkan-wide revolt against 'the unbearable tyranny' of the Ottomans. Betrayed before he had even left Habsburg territory, he was handed over, with a number of fellow conspirators, to the Ottomans, and strangled in Belgrade in May 1798. Although his mission was a total failure, he thoroughly alarmed the Ottoman authorities, whose complacent indifference to the French Revolution and its European consequences had been shattered by the revolutionary 'liberation' of the Venetian-ruled Ionian Islands in 1797. After a brief Russo-Turkish condominium, the islands passed from Russian to French and finally to British rule. In 1815 they were constituted as an independent state under British protection. If this independence proved to be more notional than real, nonetheless the Ionian Islands did afford a suggestive example to the mainlanders of an area of free Greek soil.

Rigas' martyrdom proved to be a powerful inspiration to that small but growing number of Greek nationalists who placed their faith in armed revolt rather than intellectual regeneration. Three such, Emmanuel Xanthos, Nicholas Skouphas, and Athanasios Tsakaloff, humble members of the Greek mercantile *diaspora*, came together in Odessa in 1814 to found the *Philiki Etairia* (Friendly Society), whose explicit purpose was the 'liberation of the Motherland' through an armed uprising. With elaborate initiation rituals based on masonic prototypes, and a hierarchical membership, the Society made little progress in recruiting adherents during the early years, but from 1818 growing numbers were initiated, particularly among the communities outside the Greek lands. Efforts to secure official Russian backing met with no success,

13

although the leadership was careful to sustain the myth of such support, being fully aware of the strength of popular belief in the Russians, fellow Orthodox Christians, as the most likely foreigners to liberate the Greeks. Attempts to persuade Count Ioannis Capodistrias, a Greek from Corfu who was Tsar Alexander I's joint foreign minister, to become supreme leader of the enterprise failed, and in 1820 the Society turned instead to Prince Alexander Ypsilantis, a Greek in the service of the Russian army. Complex schemes, predicated on the support of the Serbs and the Bulgarians, were elaborated, but in the event the non-Greek Christians of the Balkans showed little interest. Revolt was actually precipitated by the attempt which Sultan Mahmud II launched during the summer of 1820 to curb the pretensions of Ali Pasha of Ioannina, the Albanian *ayan* or war lord, who held sway over much of mainland Greece. Ali was one of a number of provincial magnates who ruled over large areas of the Ottoman Empire, *de facto* if not *de jure* independently of the Porte, and whose power Mahmud II was determined to crush in a concerted effort to restore the authority of the central government.

The campaign against Ali Pasha, which tied up large numbers of Ottoman troops, was too good an opportunity to miss, and Ypsilantis, with a motley band of emigré Greeks and students, launched an invasion of the Danubian Principalities across the river Pruth in March 1821. Ypsilantis had hoped to exploit an uprising of the native Romanian inhabitants, led by Tudor Vladimirescu, against the local *boyars* or notables. But Vladimirescu's followers showed no inclination to fight against the Turks on behalf of their Phanariot Greek oppressors, and Ypsilantis' campaign rapidly collapsed in ignominious failure. More or less simultaneously, however, sporadic outbursts of violence coalesced into a fully fledged revolt in the Peloponnese. This was prompted by fears that the Peloponnesian primates, the traditional leaders of the Greeks of the region, were being lured into a trap by the Ottoman authorities. This uprising was to meet with much greater success. Bloody fighting, with brutal atrocities on both sides, was followed by the withdrawal of the Turks, always very much in a minority in the region, to their coastal fortresses. The Peloponnese (the southern part of mainland Greece) and the nearer islands were to be the focus of the fighting over the next few years. The Greeks' skill at irregular warfare, their command of the sea, and the mixed blessing of the arrival of philhellene volunteers from Western Europe enabled them to maintain their initial advantage in the early years of the struggle.

It soon became abundantly clear that the chronic tendency to factionalism on the Greek side threatened the whole edifice of the uprising. Within a remarkably short time, and long before the revolt was assured of ultimate success, three provisional governments had come into existence. A highly democratic constitution, reflecting the views of the Westernizing intellectuals, was adopted early in 1822, but it was not until 1823, when a second, modified constitution was proclaimed, that the concept of a single, central authority was accepted in theory if not necessarily in practice. The new central government in turn became the object of rival factions, and by 1824 a state of open civil war existed between feuding groups. The politics of the insurgent Greeks are of a complexity that almost defies analysis. The Peloponnesian primates sought to retain the power that they had enjoyed under Ottoman rule. The klephtic (bandit) leaders were determined that their vital contribution to the war effort should be rewarded with political power. The small group of Westernizers sought to ensure that Greece was equipped with all the trappings of a Western constitutional state. The island shipowners also demanded their share of power, in a society in which regional loyalties often overrode devotion to the common cause.

During the course of the struggle, political alliances and alignments constantly shifted. One basic divide in the civil strife that accompanied the war of independence was the cleavage between what has been termed the 'military' or 'democratic' party, in which the former leaders of the klephts represented, if by default, the interests of the mass of the Greek population, and the 'civilian' or 'aristocratic' party. This latter grouping was centred on the Peloponnesian primates, the notables of the shipowning islands, and the small group of Phanariot politicians who had gained their political experience under the Ottomans but had now thrown in their lot with the insurgents. The conflict can also be seen in terms of a clash between the educated Westernizers and the traditional élites that had hitherto dominated Greek society. The Westernizers thought in terms of a conscious and clearly articulated nationalism, the traditional élites more in terms of a religious war against the Turks. Whereas the Westernizers were anxious to endow Greece with all the institutions of a liberal constitutional state and to curb the political powers of the Orthodox Church, the traditional élites thought more in terms of substituting their own oligarchical rule for that of the Turks, while retaining a significant role in government for the Church.

These basic conflicts in Greek society, reflecting divisions that had already become apparent during the pre-independence period, had by no means been resolved when the military situation changed very much to the Greeks' disadvantage. This reversal resulted from Sultan Mahmud II's success in enlisting the support of Mehmet Ali, the ruler of Egypt, and of his son Ibrahim Pasha, to crush the revolt. The price of their co-operation was high, but Ibrahim rapidly established himself in the Peloponnese early in 1825 and began a relentless drive against the insurgents. As the military position deteriorated, the Greeks increasingly looked to the Powers for their salvation. The initial reaction of the Europe of the Holy Alliance to the revolt, as was to be expected, had been downright hostile. Tsar Alexander I's feeling for his Orthodox co-religionists had been overridden by his unwillingness to countenance rebellion against the established order. Gradually, however, the Powers principally concerned in the region, Britain and Russia, whose trade had been affected by the war, began to move towards a cautious involvement. The Greeks were recognised by the British as belligerents in 1823, and Canning, fearful of Russian, Austrian and French intentions in the area, successfully proposed Anglo-Russian mediation in the conflict, a move which was joined by France. This policy of 'peaceful interference' culminated in the Battle of Navarino of October 1827, in which a combined British, Russian and French fleet destroyed the Turco-Egyptian fleet and thus ensured the emergence of some form of independent Greece.

Nation Building and the 'Great Idea' 1827-1913

Count Capodistrias, who had left the Russian service in 1822, was elected president of Greece in 1827 and manfully struggled to create the basic institutions of the state in a country ravaged by years of war. At the same time he deployed all his undoubted diplomatic skills in ensuring that the boundaries of the new state were set as wide as possible. His paternalist and authoritarian ways, however, did not endear him to influential groups in the fledgling state, and he was assassinated in October 1831. Britain, France and Russia had already determined that Greece should be endowed with a monarchical form of government, and their choice of king was the 17-year-old Otto of Wittelsbach, second son of King Ludwig of Bavaria. In a separate treaty with the Ottoman Empire, the Powers assumed the role of guarantors of the new state, whose territories were to run from Volos in the east to Arta in the west. The area thus defined was so small that it left at least twice as many Greeks still under Ottoman rule as within the boundaries of the new kingdom. The result was that, from the outset, irredentism dominated both the external relations and the domestic policies of the new state, which was not to achieve its present boundaries for over a century (see map on p. 4).

Until 1835 Greece was governed by a regency council composed of Bavarians, who showed little sensitivity towards Greek aspirations and little awareness of Greek realities. Instead they sought to fashion the state after the West European model. The influence of the large numbers of Bavarians who formed part of Otto's entourage was deeply resented by the stalwarts of the war of independence, who felt that their efforts had not received their due reward. The politics of this early period of Otto's reign were focussed around loose groupings known as the 'English', 'French' and 'Russian' parties, which were closely tied to the ministers of the three protecting powers. The 'English' party attracted the support of those who most bitterly resented Otto's failure to grant a constitution, which had been a condition of the original settlement. The 'French' party also favoured constitutionalism and was identified with irredentism. The 'Russian' party, on the other hand, was most closely linked with Orthodox conservatism. Otto enthusiastically espoused the popular irredentist cause, but by the beginning of the eighteen-forties he had managed to alienate much of the political establishment of his adopted country, including the constitutionalists, those disappointed by the fact that he remained a Catholic and had produced no heir, those who felt cheated of due recognition and of the spoils of office, and those who objected to the financial incompetence and exactions of his regime.

It was the disappointments and discontents of the first ten years of independence which caused the army to intervene in the bloodless 'revolution' of 3 September 1843. This was the first, though by no means the last, occasion on which the army was to intervene directly in the political process. On this first occasion, however, the army clearly enjoyed very considerable popular support. The insurgents forced King Otto to concede a constitution which, on paper at least, was a remarkably liberal document for its day. Otto, however, ably assisted by the talented Vlach politician Ioannis Kolettis, soon demonstrated that the new constitution afforded no protection against his particular brand of 'parliamentary dictatorship'. Ballot rigging, the use of brigands to apply political pressure, and *rousfeti* or the dispensing of offices and favours to secure votes, increasingly alienated a younger generation of politicians who had had no direct involvement in the war of independence.

Despite a brief popularity resulting from his irredentist zeal at the time of the Crimean War, all the old resentments against Otto once again came to the fore. As a final insult the King openly backed Austria against the Garibaldians, an attitude that was bound to offend a people nurtured on a diet of romantic nationalism. Following an unsuccessful attempt against Queen Amalia's life, Otto was ousted in a coup mounted in Athens in October 1862 while he and the Queen were on a tour of the Peloponnese. Otto made no attempt to resist his overthrow and departed to an exile in Bavaria during which he manifested to the end an unrequited affection for his adopted country.

Although the Greeks had overwhelmingly voted for Prince Alfred, Queen Victoria's second son, as Otto's successor, the choice of the Powers was Prince Christian William Ferdinand Adolphus George, of the Danish Glücksberg dynasty, who assumed the title of King George I of the Hellenes. His dynastic connections with most of the courts of Europe were to stand him in good stead during his fifty year reign. This began auspiciously with the British decision in 1864 to cede the Ionian Islands to Greece, in the hope of diminishing the irredentist fervour that continued to dominate the country's foreign, and indeed much of its domestic, policy. In the same year a highly democratic constitution was adopted, which provided for adult male suffrage, although women were not to be eligible to vote in national elections until 1955. The politics of the early part of King George's reign did not, however, differ significantly from those of Otto's 'constitutional' period. In 1875, after a major political crisis, the King was forced to concede the fundamental principle that the leadership of the government should be entrusted to whichever politician was able to command the support of the majority in parliament, but it was some years before this important constitutional principle had the desired effect of introducing a degree of stability into the ever changing sequence of administrations. Politicians felt themselves to be under very considerable pressure to satisfy the manifold demands of their voters-cum-clients, for Greek society largely revolved around the reciprocal dispensation of favours. The only way in which politicians could hope to respond to these demands was by the relentless pursuit of office. Office was even more important given the backward nature of the economy which meant that the state was a major provider of employment. One of the problems faced by the new state was that none of the great commercial centres of the Ottoman Empire, Constantinople, Smyrna, and Salonica, whose commerce had been dominated by Greeks, had been included within its boundaries. Hence many Greeks were forced to migrate either, somewhat paradoxically, to the Ottoman lands, or to Egypt or the United States.

Meanwhile Greece, although only peripherally involved, had been shaken by the great crisis that had convulsed the Balkans between 1875 and 1878. Greece tried to exploit the crisis to further her own irredentist ambitions, but she was overtaken by events and was afforded scant representation at the Congress of Berlin. By the Cyprus Convention of 1878, Britain was granted the administration of Cyprus, which became a crown colony in 1925. The Powers at Berlin invited the Ottoman Porte to consider frontier changes in favour of Greece, but it was not until 1881 that the Porte, under pressure, ceded the fertile province of Thessaly and the Arta region of Epirus to Greece. For the next thirty years much of Greece's irredentist energies were concentrated on the struggle for Macedonia, a struggle that brought her into conflict as much with the competing nationalisms of the Bulgarians and the Serbs as with the Ottoman Porte. Initially this rivalry manifested itself in educational and cultural propaganda, but from the eighteen-nineties onwards all of the parties increasingly resorted to violence.

Although the struggle to achieve the 'Megali Idea' or 'Great Idea', the romantic notion of re-uniting all the territories inhabited by Greeks, and of re-establishing the 'City', Constantinople, as the capital of a revived Byzantine Empire, continued to overshadow the sterile domestic politics of the Kingdom, some progress was made during the last decades of the nineteenth century in the direction of political modernization. In the eighteen-eighties and 'nineties the essence of a two party system came into being, with Charilaos Trikoupis alternating in power with his arch-rival Theodore Deliyannis. Trikoupis, a reform-minded Westernizer, wished to consolidate Greece politically and economically before embarking on grandiose schemes of foreign conquest. His reforms, which necessarily involved increased taxation, sought to diminish the electoral manipulation that was an established feature of political life. Deliyannis, a populist who understood the aspirations of the common Greek more completely perhaps than any other nineteenth century politician, was an enthusiastic champion of a 'Greater Greece'. His domestic policies were directed simply at overturning Trikoupis' reforms, with the result that the political system remained rooted in clientelism and the reciprocal distribution of favours. Yet for all the manifest inadequacies of Greek politics, few politicians personally enriched themselves on the spoils of office, and a thriving press enjoyed a freedom that bordered on licence.

One of Trikoupis' main objects was to establish Greece's international creditworthiness as the essential precondition for the development of the economy. In this he was hampered by Deliyannis' enthusiastic espousal of the irredentist cause. At the time of the Bulgarian crisis of 1885, for instance, Deliyannis ordered a general mobilization which was countered by a naval blockade by the Powers. The burden on the economy was considerable, obliging Trikoupis to raise taxes which in turn gave Deliyannis a useful populist issue with which to harass Trikoupis. Moreover, during Trikoupis' last administration (1892-5), a severe economic crisis, precipitated by a collapse in the world price of currants, one of Greece's major exports, forced the government to declare itself bankrupt in 1893. One consequence of this economic distress was that many Greeks emigrated to seek their fortunes elsewhere. It has been estimated that between 1890 and 1914 almost a sixth of the population emigrated to the United States.

The malaise that afflicted Greece in the late nineteenth century, and the disparity between her grandiose irredentist aspirations and the modest means at her disposal, were devastatingly revealed by her lightning defeat in the 1897 war with the Ottoman Empire. Hostilities had broken out after the Deliyannis government had mobilised the armed forces during one of the periodic crises occasioned by the insistent demands of the Cretans for *enosis*, or union, with the Kingdom. Although Crete was granted an autonomous status, Greece was humiliated by the establishment of an International Financial Control Commission whose task was to oversee the payment of interest on her large external debts. The decade following the crushing defeat of 1897 was one of isolation and self-doubt, in which politics relapsed into their traditional pattern of demagogy and jobbery. This political impasse was abruptly ended with the Goudi revolt of 1909, which brought into power the Military League.

The foundation of the Military League reflected various currents of disaffection within the armed forces, and the impetus for its highly significant intrusion into politics arose from a number of factors. The Young Turk Revolution of 1908 in the Ottoman Empire afforded a suggestive precedent, while economic unrest, continued agitation for *enosis* in Crete, and tensions in the army occasioned by poor promotion prospects and resentment at the patronage of the royal princes, combined to prompt the Military League to demand far reaching reforms. This in turn caused the fall of the government, and its replacement by one in which real power was held by members of the League. This intervention signified the emergence of the military as a major force in the politics of twentieth century Greece. But the League was increasingly impatient at working through the existing cliques of politicians and sought instead for a political messiah in Eleftherios Venizelos.

Venizelos, a native of Crete, had already made his mark in the politics of his native island as a vehement champion of *enosis* with the Kingdom. The fact that he was not tainted by involvement with the mainland politicians, who seemed incapable of facing up to the country's problems, enabled the League to make way for him without appearing to lose face. In elections in 1910 Venizelos won a massive majority in a parliament empowered to revise the constitution. Determined to demonstrate that he was no mere puppet of the Military League, Venizelos embarked on an ambitious programme of constitutional reform, domestic renewal, and military preparedness. Provision, for instance, was made for the expropriation of the remaining large landed estates. The popularity of such measures was demonstrated by the massive parliamentary majority that Venizelos secured in further elections in 1912. By now, however, his attention was increasingly focussed on foreign affairs. The Italo-Turkish war of 1911 (which resulted in the Italian occupation of the Dodecanese Islands) encouraged the Balkan states to consider a strike against the Turks to liquidate the remaining Ottoman territories in Europe. Greece had absorbed the lesson of 1897 that single-handed onslaughts on the Ottoman Empire by individual Balkan states stood no chance of success, and clearly did not want to be left out of any scramble for Macedonia by her Serbian and Bulgarian rivals. On the other hand she was in a somewhat different position on account of the very large Greek populations not only in European Turkey but in Asia Minor, which might be threatened by reprisals on the part of an increasingly nationalistic Turkish government.

In the event, Greece was an enthusiastic member of the Balkan alliance, and joined Serbia, Bulgaria, and Montenegro in attacking the Ottoman Empire in October 1912. Enjoying a massive superiority over the Ottoman armies, the allies made sweeping gains, with the Greeks capturing Salonica just a few hours ahead of the Bulgarians in November. Greece's naval superiority enabled her to liberate the Aegean islands of Chios, Mytilini, and Samos, while Crete was formally united with the Kingdom. After a temporary break in hostilities the Greek armies were able to capture Jannina and much of Epirus, and the Turks were forced to accept the gains of the Balkan allies by the Treaty of London of May 1913. When Bulgaria turned against her somewhat unnatural allies, Greece was able to push beyond Salonica to take Drama, Serres, and Kavalla. Although her longstanding ambition to annexe Northern Epirus, a region largely inhabited by Orthodox Albanians, was thwarted when the Powers recognised Albanian independence, Greece's territorial gains during the First and Second Balkan wars were truly spectacular. Her land area was increased by almost 70 per cent and her population from 2,800,000 to 4,800,000. Venizelos had managed to forge an unprecedented degree of unity among the Greek people, and the results had been impressive indeed. When Constantine I ascended the throne following the assassination of his father George I at the hands of a madman, the old prophecy to the effect that the Greeks would again hold Constantinople when a Constantine once more sat on the throne of Hellas no longer seemed wholly implausible.

Schism, Dictatorship, Occupation and Civil War: 1913-1949

The high hopes raised by Greece's dramatic successes in the Balkan wars were to be shattered by the profound rift that split the country into two rival camps during the First World War, and by the disastrous failure of her post-war adventure in Asia Minor. Greece was to emerge from this period a country divided against itself, and the consequences of the National Schism, as it was known, were to distort the country's political life throughout the inter-war period. The fundamental cause of this cleavage was the differences that developed between King Constantine and his prime minister, Venizelos, over Greece's involvement in the First World War. King Constantine, married to a sister of Kaiser Wilhelm, and convinced of an eventual victory of the Central Powers, was a firm believer in Greek neutrality. Venizelos, on the other hand, was a passionate supporter of the Entente and was, moreover, fully aware of the implications for his country of Britain's naval supremacy in the Mediterranean. Convinced of an eventual Entente victory, and hoping to secure support for Greece's remaining irredentist ambitions, Venizelos sought to commit Greece to the Entente from the very beginning of hostilities; but Sir Edward Grey, the British Foreign Secretary, was determined to prevent an alignment of Turkey and Bulgaria with the Central Powers, and was therefore not anxious to embrace the support of a country that had recently been at war with both. When Turkey did side with the Central Powers it became all the more important to try to preserve Bulgarian neutrality.

For this reason, early in 1915, Grey held out the inducement to Greece of important, but unspecified, territorial concessions in Asia Minor, in return for the cession to Bulgaria of some of the territory Greece had acquired in the Second Balkan War. Venizelos wanted to accept the offer and also to commit Greek troops to the ill-fated Dardanelles campaign. King Constantine, however, was much more cautious, while his chief-of-staff, Colonel Metaxas, resigned in protest at Venizelos' intentions. When the King reneged on his initial agreement to commit Greek troops to the Dardanelles, Venizelos felt that he had no option but to resign. He was returned to office by a convincing victory in the elections of June 1915, which he regarded as an endorsement by the people of his pro-Entente policies, but it was not long before he was embroiled in a renewed dispute with the King. This arose out of differing interpretations of Greece's obligations under her 1913 treaty with Serbia now that Tsar Ferdinand of Bulgaria had thrown in his lot with the Central Powers. Supporters of Venizelos argued that Greece was obliged to assist Serbia against Bulgarian attack, while his opponents asserted that the treaty was not binding in the event of Great Power involvement. Venizelos won support in parliament for the despatch of Greek troops in support of the Serbs, and agreed to the landing of British and French troops in the region of Salonica. As a consequence the King called on Venizelos once more to resign.

Venizelos' second resignation on 5 October 1915 signified the total breakdown of relations between monarch and prime minister. Royalists argued that the King's action had been justified, for a wide discretion in foreign affairs had traditionally been exercised by the monarch. Venizelists felt that the dismissal of a prime minister enjoying a clear majority in parliament was flagrantly unconstitutional. The second resignation marks the beginning of the National Schism, the division of the country into two fiercely antagonistic camps, the one convinced that King Constantine was bent on preserving Greece's neutrality whatever the circumstances, the other no less convinced that Venizelos was determined to commit Greece to the Entente on some pretext or another. Venizelos now boycotted political life, and relations between the Entente and the neutralist royal government in Athens continued to deteriorate throughout 1916. Matters reached a head following a coup by a group of pro-Venizelos officers in Salonica in August 1916. This prompted Venizelos to make for the city, where in early October he established his own provisional government, complete with its own army. Although initially the Entente allies withheld recognition, their pressure on the royal government increased. This culminated in landings in the Athens region in December 1916, the most blatant of the various interventions by the Protecting Powers in the internal affairs of Greece. When the landings were rebuffed, Britain and France instituted a naval blockade of the royalist controlled areas. In June 1917 King Constantine succumbed, and without formally abdicating he went into exile. Venizelos now became prime minister of the whole of Greece and his supporters purged his royalist opponents from government positions.

Substantial Greek forces were despatched to the Macedonian front, and these participated in the successful offensive launched by General Franchet d'Espérey in September 1918. Greek troops were also committed to the anti-Bolshevik campaign in Russia. As soon as the armistice had been signed, Venizelos began reaping the reward for his unflinching support of the Entente cause. In May 1919 he received the authorisation of Lloyd George, Clemenceau, and

President Wilson to land Greek troops in Smyrna (Izmir), which like much of Western Asia Minor had a large Greek population. The landing was intended to avert a possible occupation of the area by Italian troops, for Italy had also been promised territorial concessions in Asia Minor as an inducement to enter the war. By the Treaty of Sèvres of August 1920, Greece was to occupy the Smyrna region for five years, after which the population was to opt either for Greek or Turkish sovereignty. At the same time Greek sovereignty over the Aegean islands captured during the Balkan Wars was recognised and Greece was awarded most of Western and Eastern Thrace. These and other concessions were greeted with great enthusiasm in Greece, and Venizelos' supporters boasted that he had created a Greece of 'the two continents and of the five seas'. These irredentist triumphs, however, were not enough to save Venizelos from a crushing defeat in the elections of November 1920 at the hands of a war weary electorate. His royalist opponents lost no time in recalling King Constantine to the throne, to the manifest displeasure of Britain and France.

The Treaty of Sèvres was never ratified by the Turks, for whom the Greek landings had acted as a catalyst for a revived nationalism led by Mustafa Kemal (Atatürk). Kemal was able to reach an accommodation with the French, Italians, and Bolsheviks, and it was soon apparent that Greece, which had been on a war footing for the best part of ten years, was dangerously over-extended in Asia Minor. In August 1922 Mustafa Kemal launched a massive counter-attack which rapidly resulted in a total rout of the Greek armies. Smyrna was devastated in a massive fire, and thousands of Christians, Greek and Armenian, perished. The demoralised rump of the Greek army withdrew to the islands, followed by tens of thousands of destitute and panic-stricken refugees. A two and a half thousand year Greek presence in Western Asia Minor ended in what the Greeks refer to simply as 'the catastrophe'.

This shattering defeat, which finally put paid to the 'Great Idea', plunged Greece into political turmoil. A military junta seized power, and King Constantine abdicated. Five leading royalist politicians and the military commander in Asia Minor were sentenced to death by court martial for high treason. This was a preposterous charge, for whatever their other failings there was no question of deliberate treachery. Moreover, the 'Trial of the Six' had the effect of transforming the schism between Venizelists and Royalists into something approaching a blood feud, although the immediate effect was no doubt cathartic. Venizelos was not a member of the revolutionary government but deployed his great diplomatic skills to salvage what he could from the wreckage at the Treaty of Lausanne in 1923, by which Greece forfeited virtually all the gains that she had made in the Treaty of Sèvres. By a separate convention, agreement was reached on an exchange of populations between Greece and the new Republic of Turkey. The criterion of nationality employed, namely religion, produced some curious anomalies. Many of the Orthodox Christians of Asia Minor, for instance, knew no other language than Turkish, while many of the Muslims of Crete spoke only Greek. The uprooting of entire populations occasioned untold human misery, but the exchange did remove at a stroke what would otherwise inevitably have been a cause of continual friction between Greece and Turkey. Nationalist passions had reached such a pitch of intensity that the centuries old symbiosis of Christian and Muslim could not hope to survive.

The influx of something like 1,300,000 refugees (including sizeable numbers from Russia and Bulgaria) into an impoverished Greece inevitably placed enormous strains on the social fabric. On the whole, however, the problem of the resettlement of the refugees was resolved remarkably successfully. The last of the remaining large estates were broken up and distributed to the newcomers by the Refugee Settlement Commission, chaired by an American citizen, with the result that rural society was henceforth very largely composed of peasant smallholders, a development that made for social stability if not for agricultural efficiency. The influx of refugees also had an important effect in transforming the ethnographic complexion of Greece's newly acquired Macedonian and Thracian territories, which now acquired solid Greek majorities. By Balkan standards at least, Greece had become a country without significant minority problems. The population of Athens virtually doubled and, for many decades, the city was encircled by refugee shanty towns. Those refugees with urban backgrounds were able to inject useful entrepreneurial skills into the economy. The political impact of the refugees is more difficult to assess. The newly established Greek communist party (KKE) made some headway among rootless and impoverished migrants, but, in their overwhelming majority, the refugees remained loyal supporters of Venizelos, whom they continued to regard as their liberator. The refugee vote was clearly significant in the 1923 plebiscite on the monarchy, which resulted in a two to one vote in favour of a republic.

The bitterness engendered by the National Schism and the defeat in Asia Minor ensured that the political situation remained turbulent and confused, with the military acting as arbiters of political life through their politician clients. In 1925-26 a tragi-comical military dictatorship was established by General Pangalos. This combined a sabre rattling foreign policy with harsh measures to stamp out corruption, and ludicrous decrees determining the length of women's skirts. The Pangalos dictatorship was soon overthrown by a military coup. A welcome element of stability was introduced by Venizelos' four year premiership between 1928 and 1932. His principal achievements lay in improving relations with Italy and with Greece's Balkan neighbours, and above all with Turkey, his official visit to Ankara in 1930 ushering in two decades of good relations. But, remarkable though Venizelos' diplomatic achievements undoubtedly were, he could not shield the economy from the consequences of the world slump. Greece, with her large external debts and her dependence on the export of such dispensable agricultural products as olive oil, tobacco and currants, was particularly vulnerable. In 1933 Venizelos was voted out of office by his Populist opponents, a growing number of whom began to advocate a royalist restoration. In 1933 and 1935 two attempted coups sought to restore him to power. After the second coup, with which he had been openly identified, he was forced to flee into exile in France, where he died the following year. These coups, and the purges which followed them, opened up many old political wounds and there were now insistent demands for the restoration of the monarchy. In 1935, following a manifestly rigged plebiscite, King George II returned to Greece after a twelve year exile.

The King came back with a determination to act as a conciliatory force. He promptly ordered elections, which, unlike many earlier ones, were fairly conducted under a system of proportional representation. The result was disastrously inconclusive, with Venizelists and anti-Venizelists being more or less evenly matched. The communists, who had always been on the margin of politics, were now projected to the forefront of the political stage, for their fifteen seats (in a 300-seat parliament) were essential if either of the two main *parataxeis* or groupings were to form a government. Deadlock ensued, and while the politicians wheeled and dealed, public disillusionment mounted, particularly when it was revealed that both sides had been engaged in secret negotiations with the communists. The continuing impasse facilitated the rise to power of General John Metaxas, whose undisguised loathing of parliamentarianism in general and of Greek politicians in particular had previously not won him any significant degree of popular support.

Metaxas had trained as a young army officer at the Prussian military academy, where he had acquired an abiding admiration for what he termed 'the serious German spirit', in contrast to what he considered to be the excessive individualism of the Greeks. Although hitherto on the margins of political life he was determined to seize his opportunity to try to reshape Greek society and remould the Greek character. He had been appointed minister of war in the caretaker government on the somewhat paradoxical grounds that he was less of a political figure than General Papagos. When the prime minister, Constantine Demertzis, died suddenly, King George called on Metaxas to act as prime minister. Once in power, Metaxas prevailed upon the King to agree to a suspension on 4 August 1936 of key articles of the constitution, in face of a threatened 24 hour strike called by the communists.

Although Metaxas declared these measures to be temporary, parliament was not to meet for another ten years, and Greece was to imitate the example of her Balkan neighbours in substituting dictatorial for parliamentary government. Metaxas banned political parties and vented his wrath especially against bourgeois politicians and communists. During the early part of his régime at least, he seems to have benefited from a measure of acquiescence, if not actual support, from a people thoroughly wearied of the arcane and increasingly irrelevant squabbles of Athenian politicians. He was never able, however, to build up any sort of mass movement of the kind Hitler and Mussolini had been able to develop, although he had considerable admiration for their ideologies. He shared to the full their contempt for liberalism, parliamentarianism, and communism, although his nationalism was neither aggressive nor racially inspired. Aping Hitler's Third Reich, he preached the concept of the Third Hellenic Civilisation. The first was the pagan civilization of ancient Greece, the second the Christian civilisation of Byzantium. The third, to be fashioned by Metaxas, was to synthesise the virtues of both and to perpetuate his authoritarian and paternalistic style of government. He proclaimed himself 'First Peasant' and 'First Worker', but his populist, anti-plutocratic rhetoric was belied by his practice.

For all his admiration of totalitarian governments elsewhere in Europe, Metaxas, conscious of his country's susceptibility to British naval power and of King George's strong attachment to the traditional British connection, aligned his country unequivocally with Britain, to whom, indeed, he proposed a formal treaty of alliance in 1938. This offer was rejected, although a year later, in the wake of the Italian invasion of Albania, Britain did offer Greece a guarantee of her territorial integrity.

When the Second World War broke out in September 1939 Metaxas sought to preserve a benign neutrality towards Britain. At the same time he turned a blind eye towards a series of increasingly blatant Italian provocations, which culminated in the sinking of the cruiser Elli, anchored off the island of Tinos for the Feast of the Assumption in August 1940. But he could not ignore a humiliating Italian ultimatum delivered in the middle of the night of 28 October. Metaxas rejected this out of hand, the Italians invaded, and in a great wave of national exaltation the Greeks sank their political differences to unite against the invaders. Within a matter of weeks the Italians had not only been expelled from Greek territory but the Greek army had counter-attacked deep into Albanian territory, its advance halted only by atrocious weather conditions. Although it is now clear that the disparity in men and equipment between the Greeks and the Italians was by no means as great as it appeared at the time, the spectacle of the Greek David worsting the Italian Goliath was an immense encouragement to the anti-Axis struggle during the dark winter of 1940-41.

Churchill immediately despatched air support to Greece, but Metaxas was unwilling to accept combat troops for fear of provoking the Germans, who were rapidly tightening their grip on the Balkans. After Metaxas' death, in January 1941, however, his successor agreed to the despatch of a British expeditionary force, sent more in the hope of bolstering the anti-Axis resolve of the Yugoslavs and Turks than with any serious hope of checking the inevitable German invasion. When this came in April 1941 Greece was rapidly overrun, and a tripartite German, Italian, and Bulgarian occupation established.

It was not long before resistance to the occupiers got under way, the lead being taken by the communists whose long experience in clandestine activity stood them in good stead. From the very beginning there was a violent upsurge in anti-monarchical sentiment, for King George was regarded as responsible both for the Metaxas dictatorship and the horrors of the subsequent occupation, which included a terrible famine. A National Liberation Front (EAM), with its military arm (ELAS), was created, as were a number of smaller, almost exclusively republican, resistance groups, such as EDES. With the assistance of a British military mission some spectacular acts of resistance to the Axis occupying forces were recorded. But from an early stage it became apparent that the communist leadership of EAM/ELAS was as interested in securing post-war power as in harassing the enemy. EAM, much the largest of the resistance groups, sought to monopolise the resistance struggle, and in the winter of 1943-4 outright civil war broke out in the mountains between EAM and the much smaller EDES. Thanks to British intervention an uneasy peace was restored to the mountains, but it was increasingly clear by the summer of 1944 that, with the approaching liberation of the country, a desperate power struggle between the communist controlled EAM/ELAS and their opponents, republican and royalist, was inevitable.

The course of events in Greece was to be shaped, however, not so much by the internal balance of power as by the complex pattern of Great Power relations. Churchill had become increasingly obsessed by the danger of a communist take-over in a country which was traditionally regarded as being vital to British security. For this reason he was prepared to do a deal with Stalin over the division of South Eastern Europe into Russian and British spheres of influence. This understanding was finalised in the famous 'percentages' agreement reached by Churchill and Stalin at their meeting in Moscow in October 1944. Churchill secured Stalin's consent to a 90% British preponderance in Greece, in return for which the Soviet Union would have a 90% preponderance in Romania and a 75% preponderance in Bulgaria. The precise interpretation of this agreement is the subject of continuing debate, but Churchill certainly considered that he had secured what he called 'freedom of action' in Greece, and he always regarded Stalin as having been a man of his word as far as Greece was concerned. There is some evidence, as yet inconclusive, that Stalin, in the spirit of this deal, dissuaded the communists from making an outright bid for power in the wake of the German retreat from the country in the autumn of 1944, a bid which Churchill would have been powerless to thwart. As it was, the communists agreed to enter the government of national unity, headed by George Papandreou, that was created under British auspices. Returning to Greece with a small British force in October 1944, Papandreou and his associates carefully refrained from landing on a Tuesday, always a day of ill-omen in the Greek world as the day on which Constantinople fell to the Turks.

In spite of the presence of communists in the new government, no agreement could be reached with the leadership of EAM/ELAS over the demobilisation of the guerrilla forces, and by the beginning of December fierce fighting had broken out in Athens between communist guerrillas and the meagre forces, part Greek and part British, at the disposal of the national government. ELAS's objectives in launching this insurgency are not fully clear. It seems that, at this stage at least, the leadership of the left was aiming to undermine the stability of the Papandreou government so as to facilitate a quasi-constitutional road to power such as was later followed by the communists in Czechoslovakia. The massive reinforcement of British forces led to the British gaining the upper hand militarily, and an impulsive visit by Churchill and Eden to Athens on Christmas Eve, 1944, prepared the way for an armistice agreement that was not entirely unfavourable to the left, but the peace which ensued proved to be transient. The right now engaged in a campaign of terror against the left, which boycotted the elections of March 1946, the first to be held since 1936. This abstention resulted in a massive victory for the right wing Populists. Six months later, a referendum, which could not be regarded as a fair reflection of public opinion, led to the return of King George II, who had left Greece in 1941. The elections exacerbated rather than resolved the continuing political crisis, and in the summer of 1946 Greece gradually drifted towards civil war. This became a reality with the foundation in the autumn of the same year of the communist controlled Democratic Army.

With the support of Greece's communist neighbours, Yugoslavia,

Bulgaria, and Albania, the Democratic Army was able to maintain an effective campaign of guerrilla warfare, although none of the Eastern bloc countries recognised the Provisional Democratic Government of Greece that was set up in the mountains in December 1947. The British authorities, which had been more or less running Greece since 1944, precipitately abandoned their long standing protectorate over Greece in March 1947. President Truman took up the challenge and proclaimed the Truman Doctrine, whereby the United States guaranteed support for governments which were threatened with armed subversion. This resulted in a massive programme of military and economic aid to a Greece that had scarcely begun to recover from the ravages of war and occupation.

Although the national government was hard pressed throughout much of 1948, the tide began to turn slowly against the Democratic Army. The flow of American military equipment, and the expertise of American military advisers, helped to restore the morale of the beleaguered national army. Internal dissension undermined the military potential of the Democratic Army, and in 1948 its commander, Markos Vafiadis, who favoured classic guerrilla tactics, was ousted by Nikos Zakhariadis, the secretary general of the Greek Communist Party (KKE), who favoured set piece confrontations with an increasingly better trained and equipped national army. Moreover, international factors, as so often before in Greece's history, were to have a decisive influence on the outcome of the civil war. The KKE sided with the Kremlin in its quarrel with Tito in 1948, and so the Yugoslav frontier was closed in 1949, a move which cut the Democratic Army off from its primary source of logistic support. Following fierce battles in the summer of 1949 the remnants of the Democratic Army fled into exile in Eastern Europe.

Authoritarian Democracy, Military Dictatorship and Political Renewal: 1949-1981

The end of the civil war ushered in a confused period of coalition government. Serious progress towards reconstruction began only under the right wing government of Marshal Papagos between 1952 and 1955. Papagos was succeeded in 1955 by Constantine Karamanlis who for the next eight years headed a conservative National Radical Union government. It was during this period that the foundations were laid for the high rate of economic growth that has characterised the economy in the post-war period. Yet although the country prospered, there were great disparities in the distribution of income, and the economy was unbalanced, with the bulk of investment being channelled into property and service industries. The development process was also accompanied by a dramatic flight from the countryside to the towns, with the result that by the beginning of the nineteen-eighties more than a third of the entire population of Greece was concentrated in the area of Greater Athens.

It was under the Karamanlis government that a solution, albeit temporary, to the violent demands for the union of Cyprus with Greece was found, by creating the independent state of Cyprus in 1960. But discontent increased with the continuance of the repressive legislation that had been enacted during the civil war to contain the communist threat. Demands for greater liberalisation were in part a consequence of the massive urbanization that was such a characteristic feature of the post-war period. In the early 1960s they resulted in a break in the post-war monopoly of power enjoyed by the right.

In November 1963, George Papandreou, the leader of the Centre Union, won a narrow victory at the elections, and Karamanlis went into a self-imposed exile in France. In further elections in February 1964, Papandreou's Centre Union won a convincing majority in parliament and embarked on a moderately reformist programme. Within a short time, however, Papandreou was embroiled in a major constitutional conflict with the young King Constantine II, who had succeeded his father King Paul in 1964. The political crisis of July 1965, which resulted in the resignation of Papandreou as prime minister, was the prelude to a period of acute political instability. This was to afford the pretext, on 21 April 1967, for a small group of ultra right wing officers to mount a coup d'état whose purpose was to pre-empt elections which Papandreou was widely expected to win, and to avert an alleged but mythical threat of a communist take-over of the country. The Colonels' regime, as it came to be known, was an anachronism, offering little in the way of ideology save an undisguised contempt for politicians, a virulent anti-communism, and a populist rhetoric that was consistently belied in practice. For seven and a half years it kept a firm grip on power, using harsh measures against its opponents. Although manifestly unpopular, the régime was brought down not as a result of pressure from below but as the result of an ill-conceived coup to depose President Makarios of Cyprus and bring about the *de facto*, if not *de jure*, union of the island with Greece. This clumsy move provoked a Turkish invasion of the island in July 1974 and precipitated the collapse of the military régime. This disintegrated under the weight of its own manifest incompetence and in a state of total international isolation.

Constantine Karamanlis was summoned back from France to liquidate the legacy of a dictatorship that was as brutal as it was inefficient. His primary task was to ensure that the army not only returned to barracks but that it stayed there: his second was to defuse the massive upsurge in anti-American sentiment that swept the country in the aftermath of the collapse of the Colonels. (The American administration was seen as having been the principal external prop of the Colonels' régime and as bearing a major responsibility for the tragedy of Cyprus). A referendum on the future of the monarchy in 1974 resulted in a two to one vote against a return of the King, and a new constitution, which manifested considerable Gaullist influences, was enacted in 1975. Karamanlis won convincing victories in elections in 1974 and 1977. On the domestic front one of his most remarkable measures was to legalise the Communist KKE, officially banned since 1947. He now sought to integrate the far left into the political system rather than to isolate it as had been his policy in the 1950s and early '60s. His main attention, however, was focussed on securing the rapid accession of Greece to the European Economic Community. It was argued that such a move would compensate for the country's poor relations with the United States, her traditional patron, and afford protection against any possible aggression from Turkey, with whom relations continued to be difficult. It was also claimed that Greece's entry into the EEC would bring not only economic benefits but also serve to consolidate Greece's newly re-acquired political freedoms. This drive for membership had a successful outcome with the signing in May 1979 of Greece's Treaty of Accession to the European Community, which provided for full membership of the Community in January 1981. Having secured this long cherished ambition, Karamanlis was elected president of Greece for a five year term in May 1980.

In January 1981, then, Greece stood poised on the verge of one of the most significant stages of her independent history. Whether membership of the European Economic Community, which in a sense symbolised the healing of a 1,000 year breach with Western Christendom, would prove the kind of universal panacea for the country's economic, political, and social problems that its protagonists argued, remained to be seen. But certainly the remarkable smoothness of the transition from dictatorship to a genuine pluralistic democracy gave cause for some optimism that the country was heading for a period of greater political and social stability than she had so far experienced in the century and a half since her first independence from the Ottoman Turks. The measure of the country's progress in recent years could be seen by contrasting her political freedoms and material benefits with those of her immediate neighbours who shared her heritage of Ottoman rule and in some cases of Orthodox Christianity. The contrast was not to Greece's disadvantage.

Bibliography

Starred works contain extensive bibliographies. Preference has been given to works that are likely to be readily accessible. The three recent and up-to-date introductions to Modern Greek history are John CAMPBELL and Philip SHERRARD, *Modern Greece* (1968)★; C. M. WOODHOUSE, *The Story of Modern Greece* (1968, 2nd ed. 1977) and Richard CLOGG, *A Short History of Modern Greece* (1979)★. The story of the evolution of the modern Greek state is told in Douglas DAKIN, *The Unification of Greece 1770-1923* (1972)★. The fall of the Byzantine Empire and the period of Ottoman rule are covered in D. M. NICOL, *The Last Centuries of Byzantium 1261-1453* (1972)★; Steven RUNCIMAN, *The Fall of Constantinople 1453* (1965); D. A. ZAKYTHINOS, *The Making of Modern Greece: from Byzantium to Independence* (1976); Steven RUNCIMAN, *The Great Church in Captivity: a study of the Patriarchate of Constantinople from the eve of the Turkish Conquest to the Greek War of Independence* (1968)★; and Richard CLOGG, *The Movement for Greek Independence 1770-1821: a collection of documents* (1976)★.

C. W. CRAWLEY, *The Question of Greek Independence: a study of British Policy in the Near East, 1821-1833* (1930) treats of the War of Independence in its international setting, while Douglas DAKIN, *The Greek Struggle for Independence 1821-1833* (1973)★ concentrates more on its military and political aspects. C. M. WOODHOUSE, *Capodistria: the Founder of Greek Independence* (1973)★ is a thorough study of the first president of Greece. The politics of the early years of the independent state are fully covered in John Anthony PETROPULOS, *Politics and Statecraft in the Kingdom of Greece 1833-1843* (1968)★. The important church settlement of the early years of King Otto's reign is studied by Charles A. FRAZEE, *The Orthodox Church and Independent Greece 1821-1852* (1969). No recent study of the politics and society of later 19th century Greece exists in English, although these matters are interestingly touched on in Romilly JENKINS, *The Dilessi Murders* (1961). A crucial period in Greece's pursuit of the 'Great Idea' is discussed by Evangelos KOFOS, *Greece and the Eastern Crisis 1875-1878* (1975). The Macedonian question is the subject of Douglas DAKIN, *The Greek Struggle in Macedonia 1897-1913* (Salonica 1966). The Goudi coup of 1909, a major turning point in 20th century history, is described in Victor PAPACOSMA, *The Military in Greek Politics* (1977), while George LEON examines the crucial period of the First World War in *Greece and the Great Powers 1914-1917* (1973). The disastrous Anatolian entanglement is recounted in Michael LLEWELLYN SMITH, *Ionian Vision: Greece in Asia Minor 1919-1922* (1973).

John KOLIOPOULOS analyses Britain's relations with Greece on the eve of World War II in *Greece and the British Connection 1935-1941* (1977). The attempted Italian invasion of

Greece is the subject of Mario CERVI, *The Hollow Legions: Mussolini's blunder in Greece, 1940-1941* (London 1971). The critical period of the Axis occupation and subsequent civil war is analysed in John IATRIDES, *Revolt in Athens: the Greek Communist 'Second Round', 1944-1945* (1972) and C. M. WOODHOUSE, *The Struggle for Greece 1941-1949* (1976)★. Useful for an understanding of the rapid pace of development in post-war Greece are W. H. McNEILL, *The Metamorphosis of Greece since World War II* (1978) and Nicos MOUZELIS, *Modern Greece: facets of underdevelopment* (1978). Richard CLOGG and George YANNOPOULOS, eds., *Greece under Military Rule* (1972)★ covers the early part of the Colonels' dictatorship. A comprehensive annotated listing of works on all aspects of Modern Greece is contained in Richard and Mary Jo CLOGG, *Greece* (Oxford 1981).